FUN FACT FILE: ANIMALS!

20 FUN FACTS ABOUT PENGUINS

By Heather Moore Niver

Gareth Stevens
Publishing

Please visit our website, www.garethstevens.com. For a free color catalog of all our high-quality books, call toll free 1-800-542-2595 or fax 1-877-542-2596.

Library of Congress Cataloging-in-Publication Data

Niver, Heather Moore.
20 fun facts about penguins / Heather Moore Niver.
    p. cm. — (Fun fact file. Animals!)
Includes index.
ISBN 978-1-4339-6523-4 (pbk.)
ISBN 978-1-4339-6524-1 (6-pack)
ISBN 978-1-4339-6521-0 (library binding)
1. Penguins—Juvenile literature. I. Title. II. Title: Twenty fun facts about penguins.
QL696.S473N58 2012
598.47—dc23

                            2011036006

First Edition

Published in 2012 by
Gareth Stevens Publishing
111 East 14th Street, Suite 349
New York, NY 10003

Copyright © 2012 Gareth Stevens Publishing

Designer: Michael J. Flynn
Editor: Greg Roza

Photo credits: Cover, pp. 1, 5, 6, 8, 9, 10, 11, 12, 13, 14, 15, 16, 19, 20, 21, 22, 23, 24, 25, 26, 27, 28, 29 Shutterstock.com; p. 7 English School/The Bridgeman Art Library/Getty Images; p. 17 Daisy Gilardini/The Image Bank/Getty Images; p. 18 Doug Allan/Oxford Scientific/Getty Images.

Printed in the United States of America

CPSIA compliance information: Batch #CW12GS: For further information contact Gareth Stevens, New York, New York at 1-800-542-2595.

Contents

Words in the glossary appear in **bold** type the first time they are used in the text.

Swimming Birds?

It's hard not to smile when you see a penguin. They waddle around in a funny way. They look like they're having so much fun when they slide along the ice on their bellies. And they look like they're wearing black-and-white suits!

But did you know their coloring serves a purpose? It helps keep them safe from enemies. Did you know penguins slide because it's the fastest way for them to get around on land? Did you know that they're amazing swimmers?

Penguins have webbed feet.
This helps them swim fast.

Birds That Don't Fly

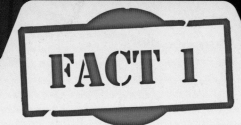

FACT 1

Penguins have wings, but they can't fly.

Penguins are birds. However, they can't fly like most birds can. Penguin wings are more like boat paddles! Their wings are **flippers** that help them swim. They're covered with stiff feathers that are kind of like a fish's scales.

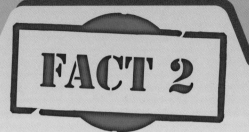
A long time ago, penguins flew just like other birds.

Millions of years ago, penguins could fly like other birds. They used to have regular feathers on their wings. For many years, they hardly ever used their wings. Because of this, penguin wings became smaller, their feathers changed, and they couldn't fly at all.

The great auk, shown here, was a close relative of the penguin. The last great auks died out during the 1800s.

7

Penguins Then and Now

FACT 3

Penguins used to be taller than some adult humans!

Back in **prehistoric** times, some penguins were 6 feet (1.8 m) tall! These days, the tallest penguin is the emperor penguin. It's only 3 1/2 feet (1.1 m) tall. The fairy penguin is the smallest at only 16 inches (41 cm) tall.

fairy penguin

crested
penguin

There are 17 different kinds of penguins.

There are 17 species, or kinds, of penguins. They're sorted into six groups. Crested penguins have fancy feathers over their eyes. Penguins with long, stiff tails are part of the brush-tailed group. Other groups are banded, large, yellow-eyed, and little penguins.

Name	Scientific Name	Height
Adélie	*Pygoscelis adeliae*	18–24 inches (46–61 cm)
African	*Spheniscus demersus*	24–28 inches (61–71 cm)
chinstrap	*Pygoscelis antarctica*	18–24 inches (46–61 cm)
emperor	*Aptenodytes forsteri*	44 inches (112 cm)
erect-crested	*Eudyptes sclateri*	25 inches (64 cm)
fairy	*Eudyptula minor*	16 inches (41 cm)
Fiordland crested	*Eudyptes pachyrhynchus*	24 inches (61 cm)
Galapagos	*Spheniscus mendiculus*	21 inches (53 cm)
gentoo	*Pygoscelis papua*	24–30 inches (61–76 cm)

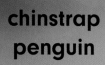

chinstrap penguin

Magellanic penguins, like this one, nest in the South American countries of Argentina and Chile.

Name	Scientific Name	Height
Humboldt	*Spheniscus humboldti*	22–26 inches (56–66 cm)
king	*Aptenodytes patagonicus*	37 inches (94 cm)
macaroni	*Eudyptes chrysolophus*	20–24 inches (51–61 cm)
Magellanic	*Spheniscus magellanicus*	24–28 inches (61–71 cm)
rockhopper	*Eudyptes chrysocome*	16–18 inches (41–46 cm)
royal	*Eudyptes schlegeli*	26–30 inches (66–76 cm)
Snares Island	*Eudyptes robustus*	25 inches (64 cm)
yellow-eyed	*Megadyptes antipodes*	30 inches (76 cm)

Note: Some scientists argue there's one more kind of penguin—the white-flippered fairy penguin, or *Eudyptula albosignata*.

Moving It

Penguins slide around on their bellies a lot.

Penguins spend most of their time in the water. On land, they face problems moving around. Their short legs don't work very well for walking. Often, they slide on their bellies to get around. They can go quite fast by using their wings and feet to push themselves along.

These gentoo penguins of Antarctica are traveling on one of their many roads.

FACT 6

Penguins build "highways."

Walking isn't a penguin's most graceful way of traveling. To make walking on snow easier, penguins pack it down to create roads that are kind of like our highways. They make hundreds of connecting roads.

FACT 7

Penguins live where it's very cold.

Penguins can be found on every **continent** of the Southern Hemisphere, mostly in places where it can get very cold. They like to build their homes on islands and in faraway areas. Few **predators** live near penguins. Some penguins travel a long way when they **migrate** to nesting areas.

Oh, Baby!

A gentoo penguin keeps its egg warm.

Penguins build their nests on the ground.

Penguins build nests out of pebbles, mud, and plants on the ground. Each year, the mother lays one or two white eggs. Both parents take turns sitting on the eggs to keep them warm. One parent sits while the other gets food.

King penguin chicks grow quickly. Some are as big as their parents before they're a year old.

FACT 9

Most baby penguins are born with feathers.

When a baby penguin is ready to hatch, it **pips** a hole in the egg's shell. Then it chips its way out, which may take 3 days! Most are born with feathers, but baby king penguins don't get feathers until weeks later.

FACT 10

Mother emperor penguins may travel up to 50 miles (80 km) to find food.

Emperor penguins have their babies in the Antarctic. A few weeks after **mating**, the mother lays one egg. She leaves the egg with the father and travels as far as 50 miles (80 km) to get food for her family.

FACT 11

Emperor penguin fathers care for the egg.

While mom is getting food, the dad balances the egg on his feet. He keeps it warm beneath his **brood pouch**. Emperor penguin dads do this for about 65 days. They don't eat until the mom comes back!

brood pouch

FACT 12

Penguins throw up food to feed their babies.

Just like human babies, baby penguins need a lot of help from their parents. Baby penguin feathers aren't waterproof, so they don't swim for their first year. The parents feed them by **regurgitating** food.

Super Swimmers

FACT 13

Penguins are the best swimmers of all birds.

Penguins are great swimmers! Their feathers keep them warm and dry. Their smooth bodies help them zip through the water. Penguins use their flippers to swim, and their feet help them steer. They can swim faster than 25 miles (40 km) an hour.

Penguins can jump as high as 6 feet (1.8 m) from the water to a rock or iceberg.

Dinnertime!

Penguins only know how to eat in the water.

Penguins spend so much time in the water that they eat there, too. In fact, when penguins are kept in zoos, they have to learn how to eat on land! Most penguins like to feast on fish, squids, and **krill**.

A penguin catches its food in its beak and gulps it down whole!

FACT 15

Hundreds of thousands of penguins live in the same place at the same time.

Penguins are very social animals. They live in groups, or colonies. When it's time for penguins to lay their eggs, they all go ashore. They build their nests in huge colonies called rookeries. Hundreds of thousands of penguins might gather together!

Lookin' Good!

FACT 16

A penguin's "suit" helps it hide from danger.

Penguins look cute in their black-and-white "suits." These colors help keep them safe from predators while in water. From below, their white bellies make them hard to see against the bright sunlight. From above, their black backs help them blend in with the deep, dark water.

Penguins stay warm by cleaning their feathers.

They're really not all that proud, but penguins **preen** at lot. A gland near the penguin's tail makes an oil. When they preen, penguins spread the oil through their feathers. Oiled feathers keep warmth in and cold out.

Penguin Talk

Each penguin has a different voice.

Penguins have a few ways of talking to each other. Of course, they use their voices to make sounds. Each penguin has its own call, or vocalization. This helps penguins know their mates and babies, because penguins look so much alike!

FACT 19

Penguins use their bodies to "talk," too.

Penguins talk with their bodies by moving in certain ways, called displays. Sometimes they display to let other penguins know where their nests are and who their mates are. Other times they do this to let other penguins know when danger is around.

Penguins have a special vocalization they use when they display, called a contact call.

Let's Keep Penguins Around

Nations around the world have agreed to help keep penguins safe.

Three kinds of penguins are in danger of dying out. For hundreds of years they have been hunted for their eggs, skin, and feathers. This has made their populations very small. In 1959 and 1991, 12 nations agreed to keep Antarctica and its penguins safe from harm.

Since 1969, it has been against the law to harvest, or collect, penguin eggs.

Tough Birds!

Penguins are cute, funny little animals. But they're tough birds! They have to be strong to live in some of the coldest areas on the planet. Not too many animals can stand such cold, snow, and wind.

Only a few people are lucky enough to see penguins in their natural surroundings. Zoos are great places to learn even more about these black-and-white swimmers and see them up close.

Chinstrap penguins gather on an iceberg in Antarctica.

Glossary

brood pouch: a pocket or hollow part of an animal's body where eggs are kept warm and safe

continent: one of the seven main areas of land on Earth

flipper: a wide flat "arm" used for swimming

krill: tiny sea animals

mate: to come together to make babies. Also, one of two animals that come together to make babies.

migrate: to move from one area to another for feeding or having babies

pip: to break through an egg's shell

predator: an animal that hunts other animals for food

preen: to groom, or clean, feathers

prehistoric: having to do with the time before written history

regurgitate: to bring food back up out of the stomach

For More Information

Books

Hanel, Rachael. *Penguins.* Mankato, MN: Creative Education, 2009.

Schreiber, Anne. *Penguins!* Washington, DC: National Geographic Society, 2009.

Simon, Seymour. *Penguins.* New York, NY: HarperCollins, 2007.

Videos

March of the Penguins. Director Luc Jacquet. Warner Home Video, 2005.

Websites

Emperor Penguins
kids.nationalgeographic.com/kids/animals/creaturefeature/emperor-penguin/
Learn more about emperor penguins—and other animals—with facts, maps, videos, and more.

Penguin
animal.discovery.com/birds/penguin/
Learn more about penguins with games, quizzes, and videos.

Index